ARTIST TRANSCRIPTIONS SAXOPHONE

THE Jackie McLean COLLECTION

Transcribed by Bruce Cameron Munson

Cover photo courtesy of Jackie McLean

ISBN 0-634-04642-X

HAL•LEONARD® CORPORATION

7777 W. BLUEMOUND RD. P.O. BOX 13819 MILWAUKEE, WI 53213

Visit Hal Leonard Online at
www.halleonard.com

BIOGRAPHY

Born May 17, 1931, Jackie McLean grew up in a musical home. Jackie's father John was a guitarist who performed with bandleader Tiny Bradshaw. McLean's instrument of choice actually began as the soprano saxophone, though by the age of 15 he had switched to alto saxophone. His early education on the instrument came through the tutelage of Foots Thomas, Cecil Scott, Joe Napoleon and Andy Brown. Another teacher that would influence him was pianist Bud Powell. His first significant band was a neighborhood band he joined in Harlem during 1948-49, led by tenor saxophonist Sonny Rollins, also including pianist Kenny Drew. McLean's first recordings as a sideman came with Miles Davis during the years 1949-53, on such recordings as *Dig* and *Odyssey*. These records would mark the beginning of the hard bop style of music, which was an advanced progression on bebop.

After Miles Davis, it was on to more work as a sideman in the mid to late 1950s with pianist George Wallington, drummer Art Blakey's Jazz Messengers, and bassist Charles Mingus. On October 21, 1955, Jackie cut his first recording as a leader with a quintet date for the Ad Lib label. His second quintet recording, *Lights Out*, also featured his fellow Jazz Messenger, trumpeter Donald Byrd.

In 1959, Jackie McLean acted in the off-Broadway play *The Connection*, which dealt with jazz and the perils of drug abuse. This eventually became a film in 1961. In 1967 McLean took his music into prisons, working as a music instructor and counselor. His community and social activism continued in 1968, when he took a teaching position at the Hartt College of Music at the University of Hartford. In Hartford, he and his wife Dollie founded the Artists Collective, a community center and fine arts school centered on youth.

At the University of Hartford, McLean established the African-American Music Department and Jazz Studies degree program. This program has produced several jazz artists of note, including saxophonist Antoine Roney, drummer Eric MacPherson, and pianist Alan Palmer, to name a few. From when he first came on the scene as a fiery hard bop saxophonist, to his tutelage of some of the brightest young talents on the scene today, Jackie McLean's style has served the jazz world well.

Bird Lives

from *Dynasty* (Triloka 181-2)

By Jackie McLean

E♭ Alto Saxophone

Fast Bop (♩ = 134)

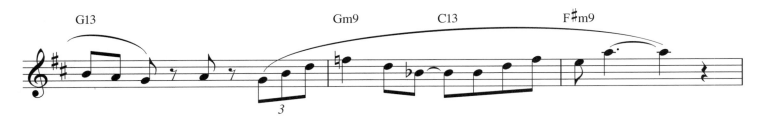

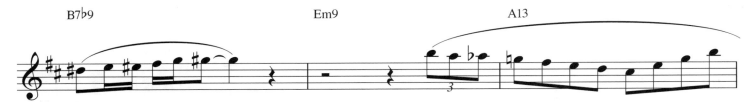

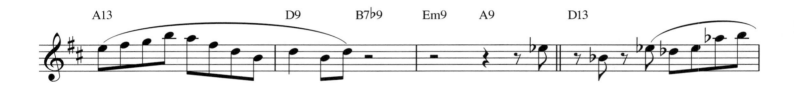

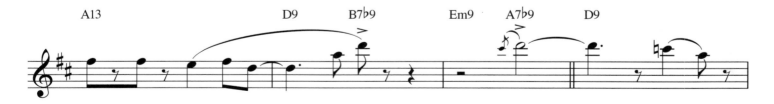

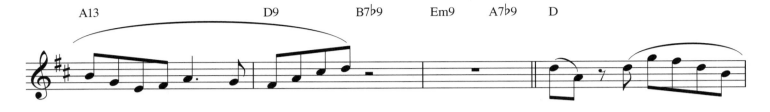

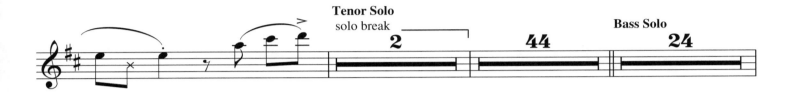

Bluesnik

from *Bluesnik* (Blue Note 84067)
By Jackie McLean

E♭ Alto Saxophone

Fast Bop (♩ = 136)

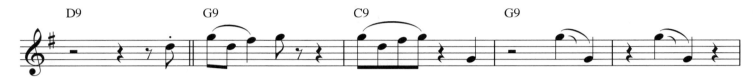

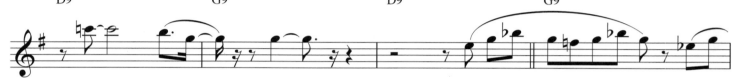

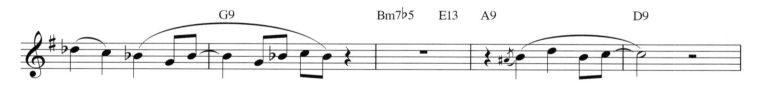

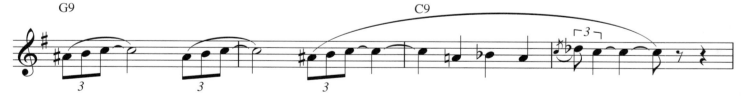

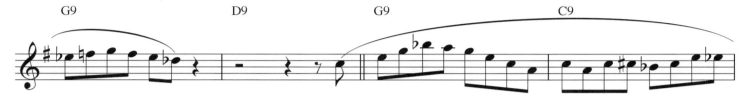

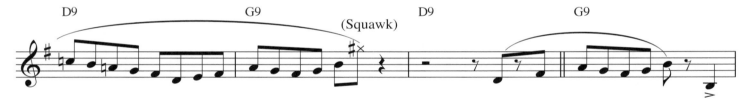

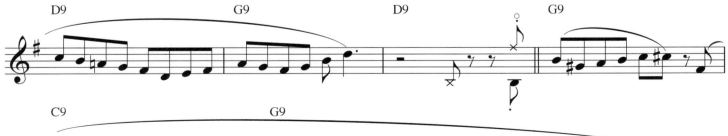

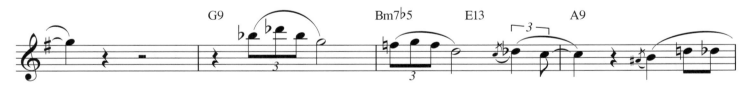

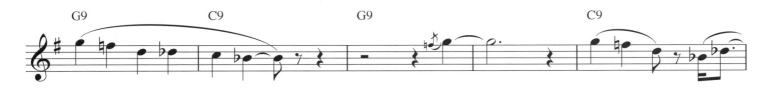

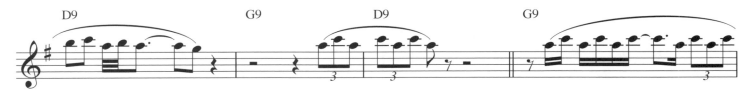

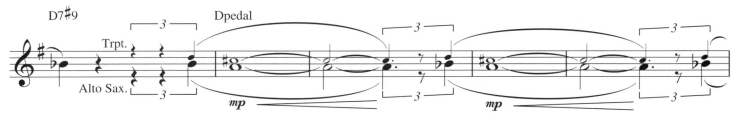

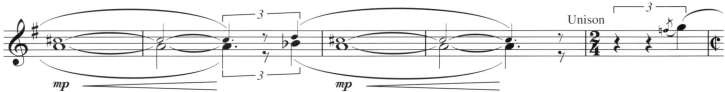

Fade out through repeat

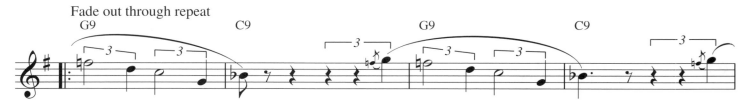

A House Is Not a Home

from *Dynasty* (Triloka 181-2)

Lyric by Hal David
Music by Burt Bacharach

E♭ Alto Saxophone

Moderate Shuffle (♩ = 120)

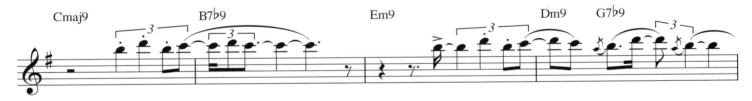

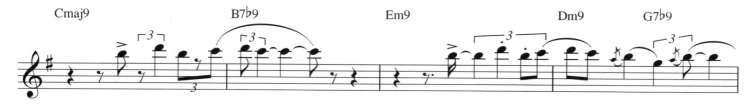

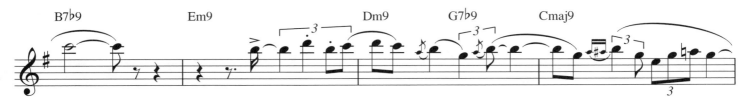

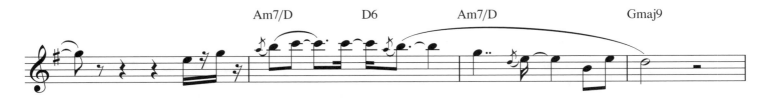

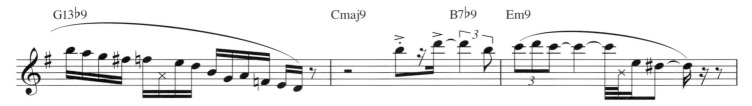

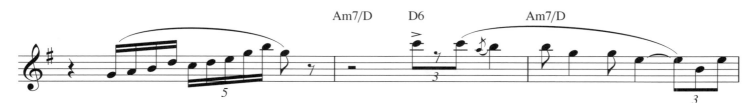

Gmaj9/D

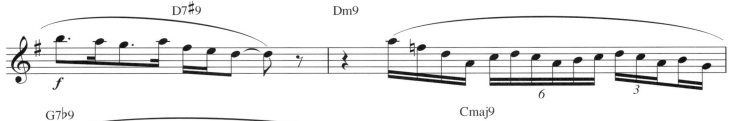

D7#9   Dm9

G7♭9   Cmaj9

B7♭9   Em9   E♭m9

Dm9   G7♭9   Cmaj9

Am7/D   D6   Am7/D   Gmaj9/D

E♭m9   Dm9

G7♭9   Cmaj7#11

A9/G

I Can't Get Started with You

from *ZIEGFELD FOLLIES*

from *Nature Boy* (Blue Note 23273)

Words by Ira Gershwin
Music by Vernon Duke

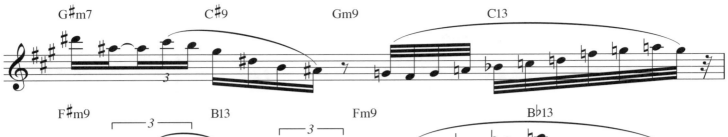

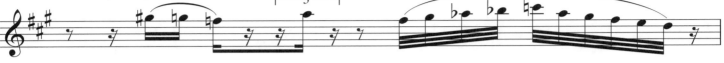

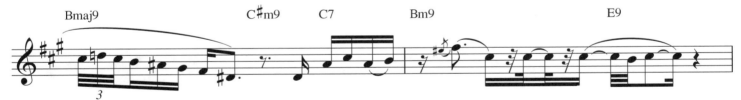

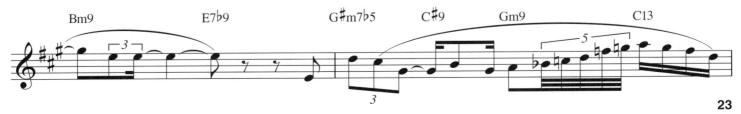

I Remember You

from the Paramount Picture *THE FLEET'S IN*
from *Tune Up* (Steeplechase 36023)
Words by Johnny Mercer
Music by Victor Schertzinger

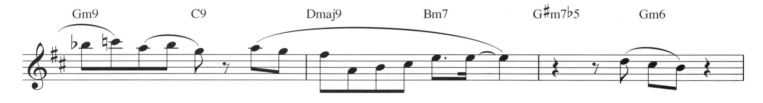

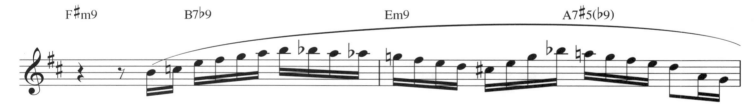

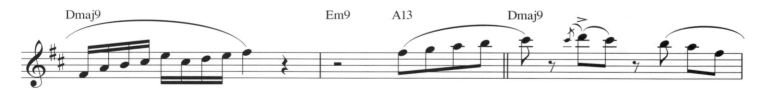

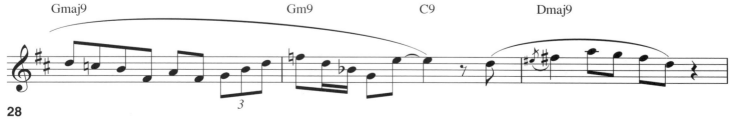

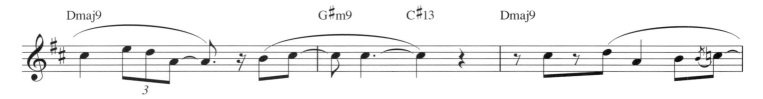

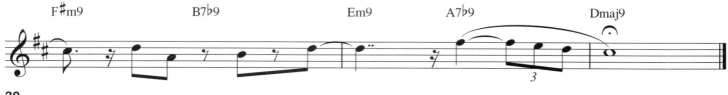

I'll Take Romance

from *Swing, Swang, Swingin'* (Blue Note 56582)

Lyrics by Oscar Hammerstein II
Music by Ben Oakland

E♭ Alto Saxophone

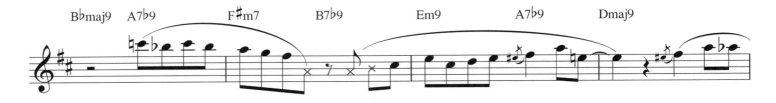

Piano Solo **95** Bass Solo **32**

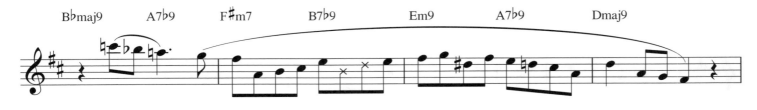

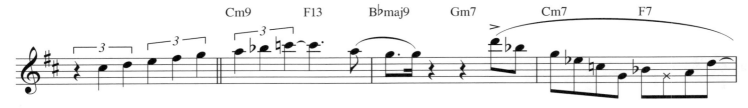

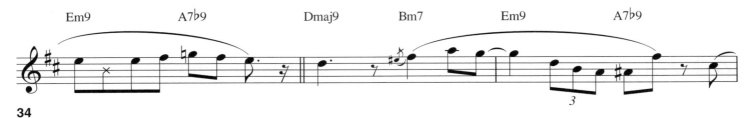

Let's Face the Music and Dance

from the Motion Picture *FOLLOW THE FLEET*
from *Swing, Swang, Swingin'* (Blue Note 56582)
Words and Music by Irving Berlin

E♭ Alto Saxophone

Fast Swing (♩ = 129)

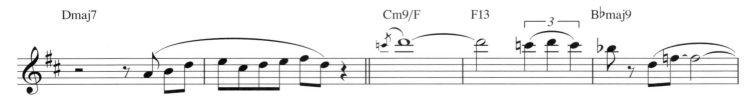

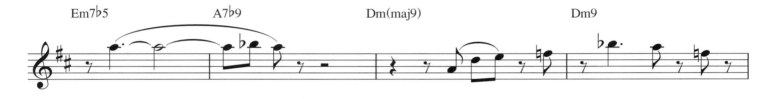

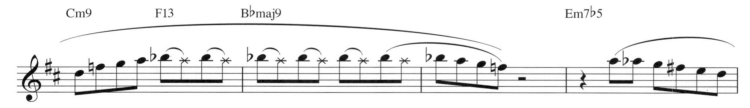

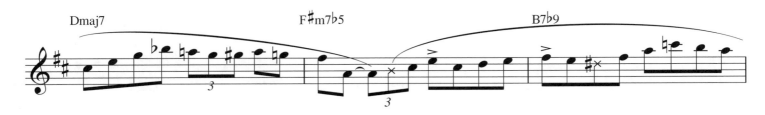

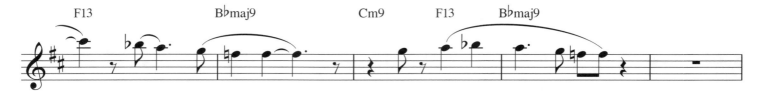

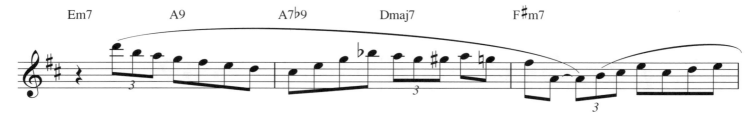

Little Melonae

from *Art Blakey and the Jazz Messengers – Hard Bop* (Columbia CL 1040)

By Jackie McLean

E♭ Alto Saxophone

Fast Swing (♩ = 220)

A13

Ab13   Ab7b5

Gm7

Ab7b5   Piano Solo
93

Ab7b5

Gm7

Drum Solo
7   F#m7b5

F9#11   Em7

A13   Ab13

47

Melody for Melonae

from *Let Freedom Ring* (Blue Note CDP 7-46527-2)

By Jackie McLean

E♭ Alto Saxophone

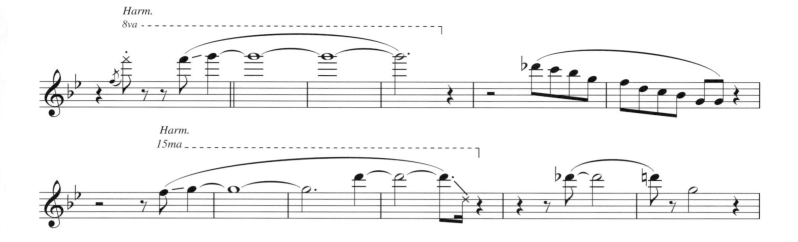

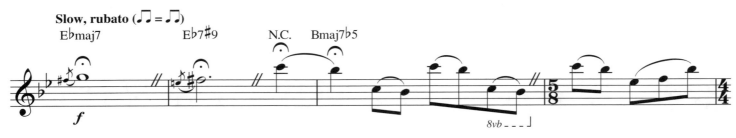

Slow, rubato (♫ = ♫)

My Old Flame
from the Paramount Picture *BELLE OF THE NINETIES*
from *Consequence* (Blue Note Classic LT-994)
Words and Music by Arthur Johnston and Sam Coslow

Eb Alto Saxophone

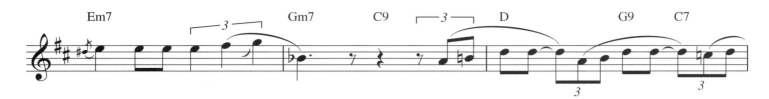

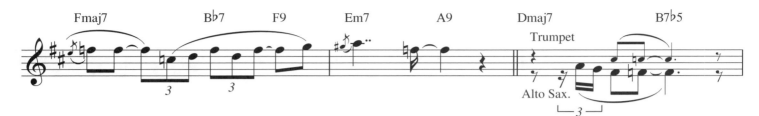

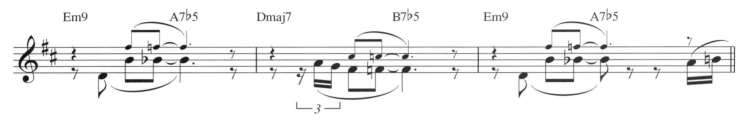

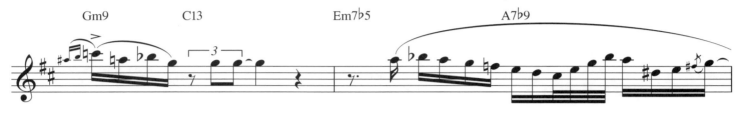

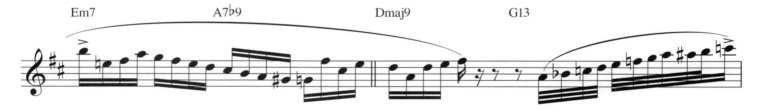

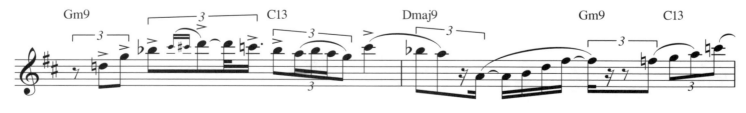

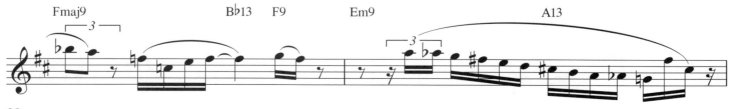

Piano Solo **15**

Trumpet Solo **8**

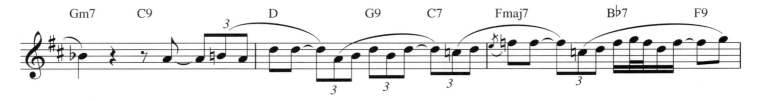

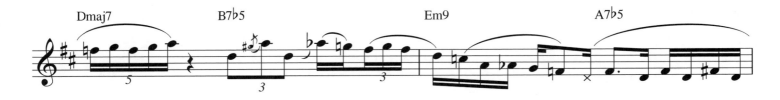

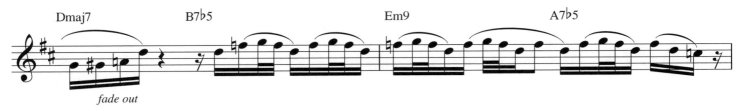

fade out

Nature Boy

from *Nature Boy* (Blue Note 23273)
Words and Music by Eden Ahbez

E♭ Alto Saxophone

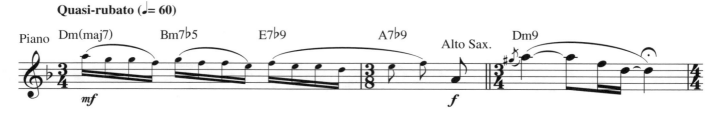

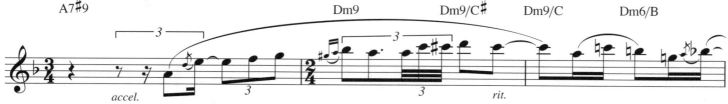

Piano Solo **75** Bass Solo **56** Bass

Alto Sax.

mf *f*

68

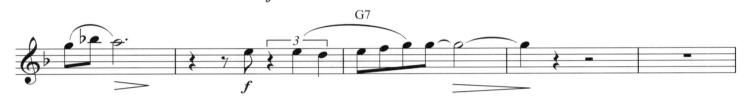

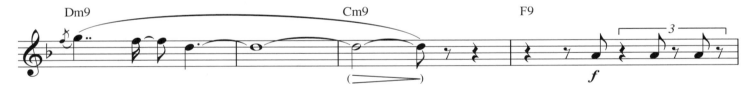

Play 10 times while fading out

A Nightingale Sang in Berkeley Square

from *Nature Boy* (Blue Note 23273)

Lyric by Eric Maschwitz
Music by Manning Sherwin

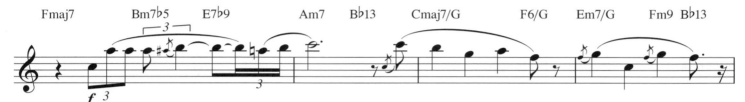

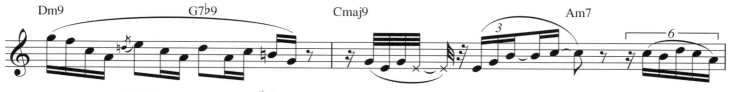

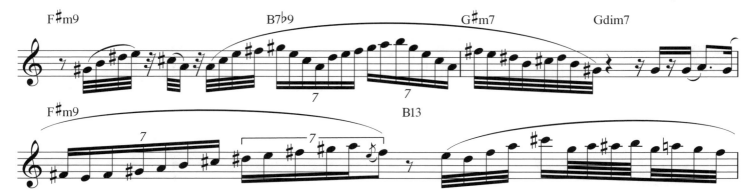

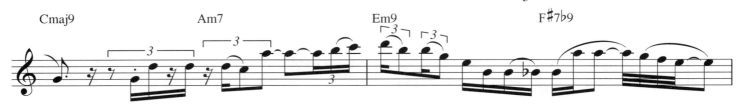

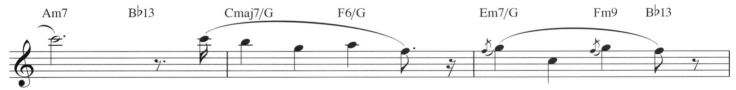

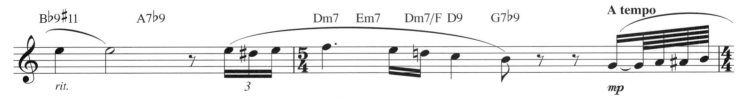

Sentimental Journey

from *4, 5, and 6* (Prestige 056)

Words and Music by Bud Green, Les Brown and Ben Homer

Eb Alto Saxophone

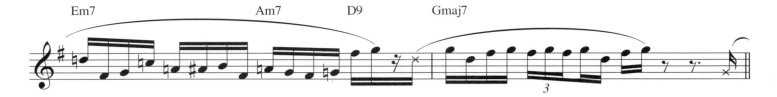

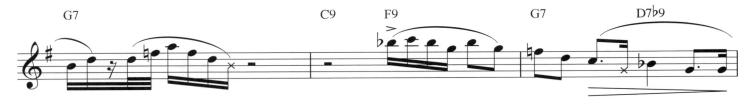

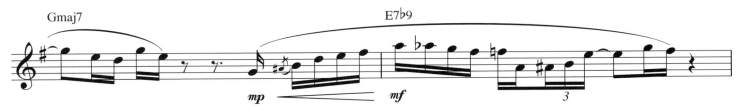

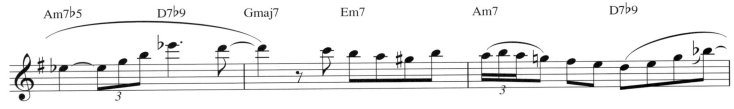

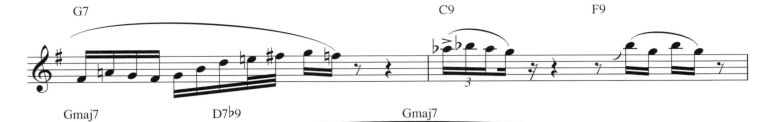

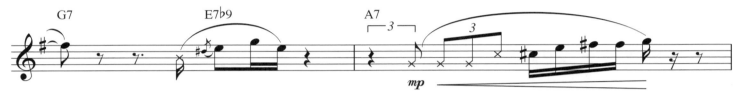

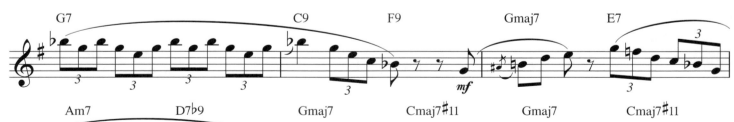

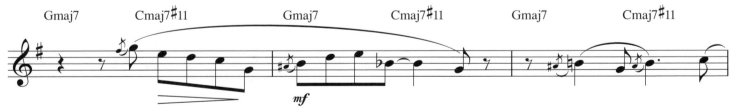

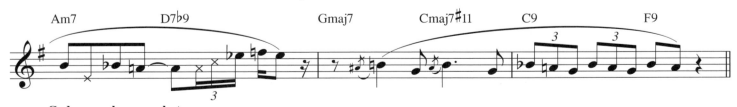

Cadenza - slower, rubato

What's New?

from *Swing, Swang, Swingin'* (Blue Note 56582)
Words by Johnny Burke
Music by Bob Haggart

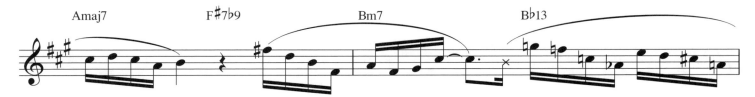

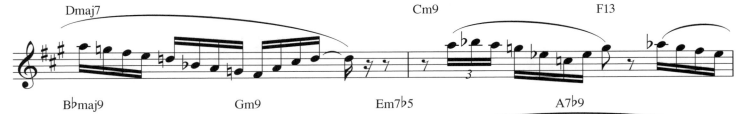

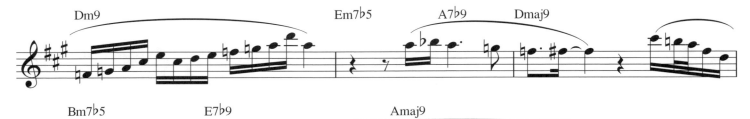

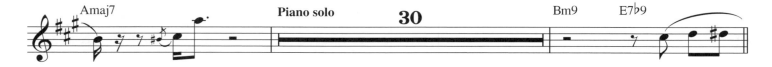

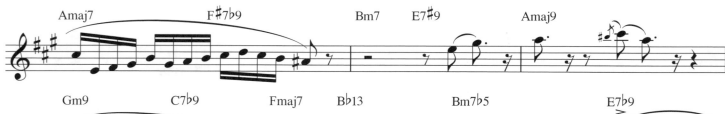

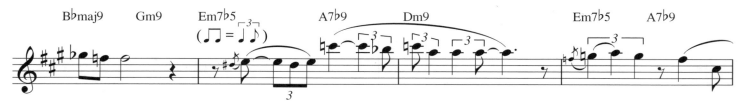

Cadenza, rubato